David and Dennis travel the world

Anna Maria Kuppe

David and Dennis travel the world

Anna Maria Kuppe

imprint

Bibliographic information from the German National Library:

The German National Library lists this publication in the Deutsche Nationalbibliografie; detailed bibliographic data can be accessed on the Internet at http://dnb.dnb.de.

© 2022 Anna Maria Kuppe

Proofreading and translation: Gabriele Kuppe
Illustrations/book cover: Anna Maria Kuppe and Gabriele Kuppe

Printed and published by: BoD – Books on Demand, Norderstedt (Germany)

English version (German version: Rabauke und Biene bereisen die Welt)

ISBN: 978-3-7557-6995-8

This book is dedicated to my beloved cats David and Dennis.

I will never forget their infinitely great love.

Hello, we are David and Dennis.

In our dreams we travel the world.

Have fun!

Table of contents

Holland/Netherlands

Their first destination is Holland, which lies on the North Sea. The symbol of the country are the numerous windmills.

"Wow!" David looks at his brother. "These big things have a lot of power when the wind blows."

"These big things are called windmills", explains Dennis and smiles at David.

"Great, that's fun. I would love to sit on these wings. Yeah! You could see everything much better from above." The little David is constantly thinking about what else he could do.

"No, please don't do that. This is too dangerous." Dennis lovingly watches over his brother so that he doesn't do too much nonsense.

"Come on, let's move on. Everything looks so colorful." Dennis wants to distract his brother a bit. Who knows what else the little joker is up to?

"Hey, there are flowers. A lot of flowers." David raises his nose to the wind and sniffs. His sweet little nose goes up and down. "That smells good!"

"Yes, these are tulips. They are very popular in Holland. This is an idyllic piece of nature." Dennis ecstatically puts his little head to the side.

"Oh, we're in Holland." David laughs mischievously. "The name sounds a bit strange."

"You can also say Netherlands. Holland and the Netherlands are the same country." Dennis heard that somewhere.

"Why can you say Holland first and then Netherlands again?" That would interest David.

Dennis was very careful. "Holland is what most people say, but in the Netherlands itself there are two provinces. On the one hand North Holland, on the other South Holland."

"Ah!" David waits a moment and thinks. "I like the name Holland."

Dennis smells the wonderful flowers. White, red, yellow tulips. These flowers come in a variety of colors and shapes. They are bred here and then sent to many countries.

The two white cats move on. Suddenly David`s stomach growls. "Oh, I'm hungry."

"I can hear it", laughs his brother.

"Where is something to eat here?" David asks and there is a new growl announces in his stomach.

"In Holland they eat cheese. Much cheese. Gouda, Edam. That's most of the products here in the country."

Dennis looks around. "There's a cheese factory. Come on, let's go."

"Cheese?" David is a little skeptical. "How does that taste?"

"Good. We can taste the cheese." Dennis marches on in the direction of the cheese factory.

"Phew, that stinks!" David grimaces. He's not picky, but now he has to turn his nose up. "Ooh, I don't like that."

Dennis means: "Come on, that tastes really good."

And David hesitates: "Well, I can really try that."

"The cheese has holes!" David looks mischievously through the many openings in the cheese in front of him. "Hello!"

"It's Leerdammer or Maasdamer, that's what this cheese is called", explains Dennis.

David stands behind the cheese. "It's funny, it doesn't stink at all like the other one over there."

Dennis continues with interest. "Come on, here is milk. Do you want something to drink?" He looks questioningly at his brother.

But David doesn't want that. "No thanks." He waves his paw and walks on.

David needs to think: "But I think we're in a cheese factory here. Why do they have milk here?"

Dennis can also explain this: "You need milk to produce cheese. This is important. Everything is made creamier with it."

"Understandable", David thinks. Then he discovers something new. There's a piece of bread in the corner. He is very curious: "Why is there still bread here?"

Dennis unfortunately has to pass. "No idea. Maybe around to taste the cheese on the bread. It can be."

Now both arrived outside and sniff the fresh air.

"Oh, that's much better. It doesn't smell that bad here. Do they eat anything else in Holland?" David loves to eat.

"The national dish is called Stamppot and consists of mashed potatoes, Vegetables, smoked ham sausage and fried onions", knows Dennis.

"It probably tastes good, but is not available here." David is a little bit disappointed.

"Then we'll drive to the capital, Amsterdam, where this meal is served definitely", suggests Dennis.

"Good idea, but how do we get to Amsterdam now?" David would like to try everything.

Dennis means: "By bicycle. The Dutch like to use it. There, look, the lady has a nice bike."

From afar, Dennis saw a nice lady riding her bike to the market.

David marvels. This woman has a bonnet on her head and wears very strange shoes.

"What is it?" Stunned, he looks at her clogs. David has to see that up close. "And people can walk in those shoes?"

The two cats rent a bike from a bike rental shop. Panting, the two reach Amsterdam. Oh, a bike tour can be very exhausting.

David and Dennis find a small, cozy restaurant by the water. There are many bridges and boats here. David watches the hustle and bustle on the river.

"These are the canals of Amsterdam. Many tourists go on excursion boats that have a glass roof." Even Dennis enjoys the wonderful view.

Lost in thought, David looks at the water. He can't get the circling blades of the windmill out of his head. "It's nice here in Holland. What else is there to see in Holland?" David finds it all very exciting.

And his brother knows the answer: "Den Haag for example. This is a town near the coast. The royal family has its seat of government here. Paleis Noordeinde. And if you love the coast, there is the beautiful holiday resort of Scheveningen on the North Sea. You can fly a kite on the beach there." Dennis heard that as a child told it.

And he thinks of something else. "If you are looking for a souvenir to take home, Delft may be the right place for you. The famous blue porcelain has been made in Delft since the 17th century."

"Are we going there now?" David secretly wishes he wouldn't have to get on a bike again.

"No, we don't have time for that. We want to see something of the world. Maybe next time."

"Phew, lucky", David thinks. "How nice that my wish is fulfilled so quickly."

The two cats move on to the next country. David and Dennis say goodbye with a polite "Daag". That means goodbye in Dutch.

Belgium

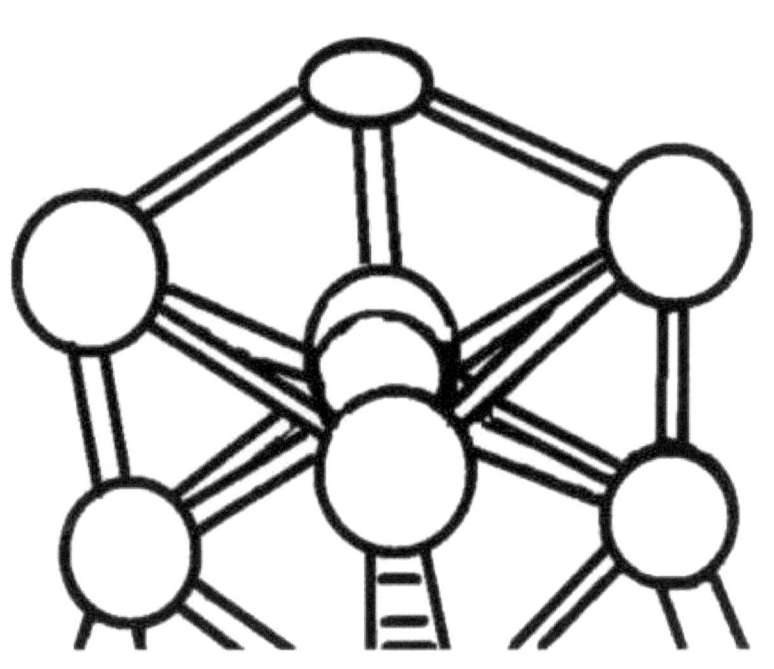

"Oh, what's that little man doing over there?" David points in horror to a figure standing in a corner.

Dennis laughs: "That's Manneken Pis, a boy urinating."

Normally David isn't a prude, but that's not possible! He can't believe it: This little thing is just standing in a corner doing his little business. "I should do that!"

Dennis can explain it: "You can say that again, but this statue is the symbol of Brussels."

With a slightly wrinkled forehead, David looks at this little figure. "But that doesn't matter, you don't do something like that."

Dennis smiles: "Yes, but this little man is very much admired. Sometimes this statue is disguised, for example at international football matches. Then they put the Belgium football shirt on this little guy or Elvis Presley on birthdays."

David turns around, shaking his head. "Oh, fashion makes this male too. But if this is art..."

His brother knows even more: "In Belgium, people love this statue very much. Many people come here to see Manneken Pis."

"So, so, we're in Belgium", David states.

"Yes", replies Dennis and points with his right paw to a place. "Look, this is the Grote Markt (Big Market). This square is a tourist attraction in Brussels. The city hall is located on this market square. In the evening the facades are illuminated. A flower market is held on the square on weekdays."

Suddenly David discovers a chocolate shop. The window of this shop is decorated with chocolates and other delicacies. "Hmm, that looks delicious." David actually loves hearty food, but he also likes chocolate.

"Come on, let's buy chocolates. It would be a shame if they were left in the shop window." Dennis doesn't say no, because he is a very sweet one.

David's mouth is full of chocolate. He smacks his lips and Dennis hardly understands a word. But Dennis also understands his brother and explains everything about the country and its people to him.

"Belgium is located on the North Sea and is a country in Western Europe. The country borders the Netherlands, Germany, Luxembourg and France. Different languages are spoken in the capital Brussels. Dutch is spoken in the north thanks to the Flemings. Through the Walloons in the south, French is more common. In the east, for example, High German is spoken."

David nods and he is delighted because he understands that his brother is very clever. "Do you know any other cities in Belgium?"

"Yes of course. Belgium has many beautiful cities, for example Knokke-Heist, Bredene, De Panne, Niewport, Oostende and Bruges. The city of Bruges is called the

Venice of the North. Or Antwerp, there is one of the largest seaports in the world."

Suddenly both stand in front of a gigantic building.

"What is it? There's a lot of bullets." David is impressed. This structure is 102 meter high.

"This is the Atomium," says Dennis. "There are 9 so-called atoms. These 9 balls each have a diameter of 18 meters. 6 balls are accessible. You can reach them by escalators. These escalators are up to 35 meters long. There are 20 connecting passages between the spheres."

Dennis could have become a teacher. Under no circumstances does he want to lecture his brother. He just wants to help that everything is better understood. But that doesn't mean that David is stupid. No, no. But for these stories, he took on that role.

This automium makes David astonish. "Wow, that's a big thing." But he just wouldn't be David if he didn't think about a little bite to eat.

"Do people in Belgium eat anything else than chocolate?"

Dennis knows that too: "Typical dishes in Belgium are Lapin aux Pruneause. This is rabbit with prunes from the Liège area. Then there are moules frites. These are mussels in vegetables, cooked in their own juice. As a side dish or just because there are delicious French fries."

The two cats find a nice restaurant and David tries the french fries.

Dennis orders the rabbit and is delighted. "Yummy, that tastes great."

And his brother wants to know: "Where are we going next?"

"Let yourself be surprised", says Dennis and smiles affectionately.

But first David has to take a nap.

That is a good thing. Eat, rest, move on.

After a break, the twins David und Dennis make their way to the next place on the discovery tour.

Luxembourg

"Hey, that's a fancy dress." David grins mischievously. A little girl is standing in front of him. She wears the Luxembourg costume. This looks similar to a dirndl.

David is curious. "Who are you?"

The girl replies shyly: "My name is Constance."

Dennis lovingly turns to the girl. "That's a beautiful name."

Immediately David and Dennis take this sweet little one to their hearts.

The two cats would like to know in which country they are. Constance willingly tells them something about the country and its people. "We are in Luxembourg. This is a so-called Grand Duchy. The Grand Duke lives here with his family. A Grand Duke of Luxembourg is also the country's head of state. Luxembourg is one of the smallest countries in the world. It covers approximately 2586 square kilometers."

David and Dennis are impressed.

Constance continues to report. "Luxembourg borders France to the south, Belgium to the west and Germany to the east. Together with Belgium and the Netherlands, Luxembourg forms the so-called Benelux countries."

That all sounds very interesting. The two cats listen attentively to Constance.

She asks hesitantly: "Shall I go on?"

David and Dennis nod. "Yes of course."

"Luxembourg is not only the name of the country but also of the capital." Constance smiles. She likes living in this country.

"What language do people speak in Luxembourg?", Dennis would like to know.

"Several languages are spoken in Luxembourg. The mother tongue is Luxembourgish, a Moselle Franconian, High German dialect. The official languages are normal German and French."

David wants to know a lot more. "And what kinds of sports do people do here?"

"Soccer is the most popular sport. But also cycling", answers Constance.

"Ah, I've heard of that before. There is a cycle race called the Tour de Luxembourg and it is used to prepare for the Tour de France." Dennis listened carefully again.

David likes it more comfortable and thinks sport is stupid. "Oh no, sports. Soccer is fine. But cycling? That's nothing for me."

When you have to listen so much, it whets your appetite.

David simply has to ask the next question: "What do they eat in your country?"

"A popular dish is Judd mat Gaardebonnen. This is smoked pork with broad beans and Bouneschlupp, a bean soup with potatoes. Then there are the so-called Kniddeln. These are large dumplings made from flour, water, eggs and salt." Constance looks questioningly at David. "Did you find something?"

He has to think. "Hm, beans, better not. Then I'll take the dumplings, that sounds good."

Dennis and Constance also opt for dumplings and so the three of them enjoy it.

After a while, the new friends pass a cathedral.

"I'm meeting my mom here now. She is a believer and so am I", smiles Constance.

Dennis stands in awe in front of this building.

"This cathedral is called: To the dear woman."

"Yes, that's right." Constance is happy that Dennis knows this and adds: "The most important religious festival in Luxembourg is the Madonna Octove, which is celebrated from the 3rd to 5th Sunday after Easter. Our Lady is the patron saint of Luxembourg."

Everyone has time for a little prayer. David, Dennis and Constance enter the sublime cathedral. After a few minutes, David whispers to the little girl. "Now we must go."

The two cats say lovingly: "Au revoir", bye Luxembourg.

Austria

"Jo mei, is de pfundig." A young boy stands in front of the Vienna Prater. This is a well-known tourist attraction in Vienna, the capital of Austria.

David raises his eyebrows. "What did the boy say? I did not understand a word."

Dennis smiles at his brother. "This is Austrian German and means something like: That's great."

"Ah I understand." David finds the expression a bit funny and nudges his brother with the tip of his pink nose. "The boy is also wearing weird pants."

"Yes, these are so-called lederhosen. Boys and men in the country like to wear them. But we also have them in Bavaria", Dennis knows.

David can hardly hold back a grin. "I think that's great. And what are the girls and women wearing?"

"Dirndl", replies Dennis and points with his right paw at a girl who is wearing such a dress.

"That looks good", thinks David.

But this big thing called Ferries wheel fascinates him a lot. "Can we come along too?"

"Of course, if you want that. You are sure to have a fantastic view from the top. You can see the entire city of Vienna," means Dennis, "but we wanted to continue our world tour."

"You're right and I'm hungry now too." Oh, oh, David is always hungry.

"In Austria you can eat well and in abundance, for example apple strudel, Salzburg dumplings, Wiener Schnitzel and Kaiserschmarrn", says Dennis.

"That sounds really tasty." David wipes his mouth. You can really see how the sweet cat's mouth is watering.

Suddenly the two cats pass a Viennese coffee house. It smells like fresh pastries.

David has to go in there. "Wow, do you smell that?" He sniffs here, he sniffs there.

Both admire the displays in the cake counter.

A friendly waiter comes by and greets the two: "Grüß Gott." That means "Hello".

David and Dennis smile at the waiter and Dennis greets back with: "Servus."

Hm, his brother can`t understand that: "Why don't you say Grüß Gott?"

"You can say both to greet the people here", replies Dennis.

Somehow it doesn't matter to David, the main thing is that he can try some of the delicious food.

Quickly he decides on the Wiener Schnitzel and for dessert he likes to try Kaiserschmarrn. "What are you taking?" David wants to know from his brother.

Dennis wants to eat the same as his brother. "But do you know what we eat?"

"No, but that all sounds delicious."

"The Wiener Schnitzel is a thin breaded veal cutlet and the Kaiserschmarrn is made with flour, eggs, sugar and sometimes with raisins", Dennis explains.

"Kaiserschmarrn sounds funny. Does this name have a special meaning?" David bounces impatiently on his butt.

Dennis nods: "Yes, it has. Austria was once an empire. It was ruled by an emperor. This man's name was Emperor Franz Joseph I and one of his favorite foods was Kaiserschmarrn. Kaiser means Emperor in English."

"A great dessert." David looks around the coffee house and listens to the people. "Can you tell me more about Austria?"

"Yes gladly. Austria borders Germany and the Czech Republic, Slovenia, Italy, Slovakia, Hungary, Switzerland and Liechtenstein. The nine federal states are Burgenland, Carinthia, Lower Austria, Upper Austria, Salzburg, Styria, Tyrol, Vorarlberg and Vienna."

And David always keeps an eye on the kitchen door: "Ah, sounds interesting. But where is the food?" His stomach is already growling.

In the meantime, Dennis just keeps talking. "Austria is also called the Alpine Republic because there are many mountains called the Alps. Schönbrunn Palace is located in the capital Vienna. Here you will find a park with the oldest existing zoo, the Tiergarten."

Finally the waiter comes. Now only the hearty food is important. David won't let himself be disturbed.

The little gourmet just enjoys. Now it's time for an afternoon nap. After eating you should rest.

He rubs his well-filled stomach with relish. "I like Austria."

"Yes", nods Dennis, "but after the meal we should continue our journey. There is still so much of the world to discover."

"Baba Austria." That means goodbye Austria.

Suddenly the boy in the leather pants reappears.

"Pfiati!", he calls.

"Pfiati? What is it?"

"That's just an expression for goodbye in Austria", Dennis knows.

"Oh, pfiati", laughs David. He is tired, close his eyes and he is already dreaming of the next trip.

Switzerland

"Gruezi." Suddenly a big dog with brown/white fur stands in front of David and Dennis. He looks deep into the eyes of both of them. David isn't usually fearful, but now he's not quite comfortable.

He boldly asks: "Who are you?"

"Sali, I'm Mo, an avalanche dog. This breed is also called St. Bernards. Our breed has been the Swiss national dog since 1884."

David looks questioningly at his brother: "Gruezi, Sali? Do you know what this means?"

Dennis nods. "Yes, I know that. These are the greetings and you can say both when you greet each other in Switzerland."

"Ah, we are in Switzerland." David carefully samples this St. Bernard.

Mo is curious: "What are you two doing here? You're not allowed to climb, it's too dangerous."

Actually, David just had that in his head. But this time he stays good. "Oh no, we just wanted to look around."

Dennis carefully asks again: "Why do you think that is too dangerous?"

The avalanche dog answers friendly: "I am at home here and know every stone, but you two are strangers. We have huge mountains like the Matterhorn. This is the symbol of

Switzerland. Many people come to this mountain to photograph it."

David looks at the mountain, which is very close. Shouldn't he dare to climb it? But no, it's nothing for little cats today.

And he keeps listening to Mo: "I wouldn't recommend you to climb that high mountain. It is 4478 meters above sea level. Only experienced climbers can do that."

"Yes, yes, of course, I just wanted to take a look", means David. But he would like to know more about Switzerland.

The three make themselves comfortable on a bench and Mo continues to report: "Switzerland borders Austria, Germany, Liechtenstein, Italy and France. There is no capital in Switzerland. The seat of government and parliament is in the federal city of Bern. The six major cities in Switzerland are Zurich, Geneva, Basel, Lausanne, Bern and Winterthur."

David and Dennis find that very interesting.

But our little David is hungry again. And what question does he then ask? "What do you eat in Switzerland?"

Mo proudly answers: "Cheese fondue."

"Cheese!", shouts David and he is not very enthusiastic. He doesn't like cheese. He wrinkled his nose: "No thanks, no cheese please. What else do you have to offer?"

Mo praises another dish. "Hash browns. These are boiled, peeled, sometimes raw potatoes. They are fried with butter or lard. There is also bacon, cheese or fried eggs."

"Hm", David has to think for a moment, "no, potatoes are not really my thing either."

"It doesn't matter, we don't have to eat all the time", says Dennis.

Mo has another idea that has nothing to do with food. "I could show you something gigantic."

Dennis has become curious. "Great, where are we going?"

"To the Rhine Falls from Schaffhausen. This is a huge waterfall. The river Rhine is 1233 kilometers long and flows through Germany, Switzerland, the Netherlands, France and Austria."

When the three arrive there, David is amazed. "Wow, that's great." He is actually afraid of water, but this sight fascinates him.

After all the new impressions, the tiredness overcomes David. "Oh, I should take a nap." He lies down on the next chair and watches the spectacle from there. "A little rest never hurts, right?"

The dog is also grateful for a little break and Dennis would like to know something else. "What languages are spoken in Switzerland?"

Mo is happy to answer this question: "There are 4 official languages in Switzerland. German, French, Italian and Romansh. But the last language is rare." Then Mo gets up, it's time for him to go. "Uf widerluege."

"Please? What?" asks David. "Oh, my goodness, what does that mean again?"

"Uf widerluege" means "bye" in Switzerland. The three say goodbye to each other.

"Yes, then, uf widerluege Switzerland."

France

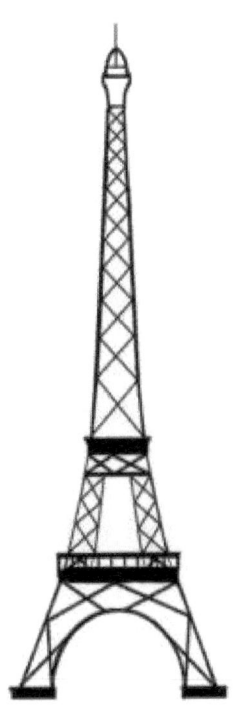

We are in Paris. This is the capital of France. Oh, la la. A gentleman with a slanted cap is looking at the Eiffel Tower. This is the symbol of Paris and all of France.

But David and Dennis have chosen a nice vantage point on the Arc de Triomphe. This triumphal arch is 50 meters high and a monument.

David looks to the Eiffel Tower. "Oh, oh, that's high!"

"Great! Phenomenal!" Dennis raves and he shines.

"Bonjour, are you tourists?", asks the gentleman with the crooked cap. This headgear is called a beret and is made of wool or felt.

Dennis nods: "Yes, we are currently on a journey of discovery through the world."

David nudges his brother: "Does Bonjour mean hello?"

With a nod, Dennis agrees. "Yes, you can say bonjour in the morning and afternoon, in the evening you say bonsoir."

"Aha." David only ever looks at the Eiffel Tower. He would very much like to climb this one.

"It is beautiful in my beloved Paris", says the gentleman. Full of joy he swings his beret through the air. "The Eiffel Tower was built by Gustave Eiffel and opened in 1889."

Dennis thinks it's great: "Wonderful. I like that. From up there you have a great view of the city of Paris. Notre

Dame, Louvre, the Seine. Just fantastic." Dennis has a travel guide of Paris and reads aloud. "Notre Dame is a cathedral and one of the most important monuments of Paris. It was built between 1163 and 1345. With its two towers, it is clearly visible. The translation means: To our dear wife and is dedicated to the mother of Jesus. Yes, and behind it is a beautiful garden. Not many people know that. It's quieter here and you can enjoy a stillness in this busy city."

David is amazed and Dennis is happy to tell more: "Montmartre is 129 meters high. There are many artists and painters."

And David is curious: "Isn't there another building like that?"

"I'm sure you mean the Louvre. This is a museum. There are many pictures on display. The most famous picture is Leonardo da Vinci's Mona Lisa", says Dennis.

"Oui", says the gentleman with the beret.

David has slight wrinkles on his face: "What did the man say?"

"That's the French word for yes", laughs Dennis and blinks in the sun. "You probably know the tennis tournaments that mom always watches on TV at home. These are the legendary french open. This is one of the four largest Grand Slam tennis tournaments and takes place between mid-May and early June at Stade Roland Garros."

At home, David`s eyes always go back and forth with the ball. "Sure, I know."

But he find the hustle and bustle on the streets more exciting at the moment. With a huge leap he takes the last step of the triumphal arch. Suddenly David is standing on a busy street.

Dennis is very worried. "Please be careful. There are a lot of cars here. The champs-Elysee, as this street is called, is very busy. You just have to be careful."

"Yes of course." Smiling David proudly walks down the Champs-Elysees. He knows his brother well.

The little gourmet is slowly getting hungry again. "What can we eat in France?"

"Baguette and cheese...", that's all Dennis can talk about.

"Oh no, cheese again!" screams his brother. He doesn't like that at all. "And baguette, what is that?"

Dennis smiles. "Baguette is a baguette. You can get that here in all boulangeries, like bakeries."

David asks sullenly. "Is there anything savory to eat?"

"Yes, in France there is even fine dining, it's called haute cuisine. Most of the time it's a lot of goodies. Unfortunately, there is often too little on the plate", smiles Dennis.

"Well, great, actually I wanted to eat normally and not something that doesn't fill me up." The noises in David's stomach just signal: I'm hungry.

He discovers a small bistro. David buys delicious chocolate croissants and ham croissants. But that should only be a small snack. David has his mouth full of chocolate and enjoys it.

In the meantime, the two cats have arrived at a river, the Seine.

"Should we go on a boat?"

"That's a good idea. This is a convenient way to discover the city of Paris. On board these excursion boats you can learn a lot about the attractions in Paris. Every tourist can understand that too, because it is told in many languages. You can take many new impressions home with you."

"Great." David has conquered a window seat and Dennis sits down next to his brother. The view is just gorgeous.

On a boat coming towards them, they see the gentleman with the crooked cap. He waves happily: "Bonjour et Au revoir."

David already gets the answer because Dennis gives it to him. "That means hello and goodbye in French."

The two cute cats wave back in a friendly way and call: "Au revoir."

Spain

The sun shines all day long and the people laugh, dance. They are happy.

"Phew, it's pretty warm in here. The sun is burning on my fur", moans David. "But it's also good."

"Yes, we are in Spain. Here the sun shines for many hours of the day." Dennis loves the country and smiles.

Suddenly, the two hear loud music.

"Oh, someone's singing weird." David pricks up his white ears, which look nice and pink on the inside. "What is it?"

"This is flamenco music."

David looks at his brother with big eyes. "Flamenco?"

Dennis is happy to explain it to him. "Flamenco is the Spanish national dance. People stamp their feet heavily on the ground, but this is their expression of joy and vitality."

Perplexed, David raises his eyebrows. "But does this man have to sing so wrong?"

And Dennis smiles. "People dream of the joy of life and express their feelings in singing."

"Great, but they don't have to make that much noise!" Horrified, David looks at the hands of the dancers. People clatter back and forth with such strange things. Somehow, he doesn't understand that.

Dennis points to the hands of the dancing people. "Those are castanets."

The little David has to think: "Well, if people think it's nice. But no matter, they should be fun and cheerful."

The smell of delicious food makes David`s nose go up and down. He quickly discovers the kitchen. "Hmm, that smells good."

He marches straight to the kitchen door. "Delicious! Chicken! But what are the cooks doing there? They throw the good chicken in a huge pot with rice and other stuff." David has to watch as the tasty meat disappears into these ingredients.

"That's paella, the national dish", Dennis knows. "The paella mainly contains rice. There are also beans, peas, tomatoes, peppers and saffron. The delicious chicken is added and seafood such as shrimp and mussels are also included in the paella."

David looks mischievously over the edge of the paella pan. "I would prefer the chicken alone. But whatever. Can I just fish out the chicken?" In an unobserved moment, he boldly grabs it.

"Ouch, that's hot!" In a flash, he takes his paw out of the pan again.

Dennis shakes his head. "You can`t wait, right?"

"No, that's taking too long for me." Suddenly, David discovers a piece of chicken that the cook left behind.

Oops, it's already in his stomach. Delicious! David grins at his brother: "Do you want a piece too?"

But Dennis declines: "No, thank you."

"You can tell me what else there is to eat in Spain." David listens intently to his brother.

"In Spain they also like to eat tortilla. This is an egg omelet. For dessert, people like to eat the Crema Catalana, a caramel cream."

"Ah, yes and does Spain have a capital?" He wants to know next.

"Yes, the name of the capital is Madrid", Dennis continues to tell. "There is a lot to see in Madrid. For example, the Almudena Cathedral, consecrated by a famous Pope or a monument on the Plaza de la Puerta del Sol (Square to the Gate of the Sun). A bear stretches out and sniffs at a strawberry tree."

Actually, David would rest again, but he's still curious. "Are we going there now?"

"No, it's much too hot today", his brother replies and wipes the beads of sweat from his forehead.

"Phew, lucky", David thinks.

"Let's move on, the next country is already waiting for us. But first we take a short nap in the shade."

Dennis agrees and cuddles up to his brother. "That's called a siesta in Spain. Since the sun is at its highest at midday, people often take a so-called siesta."

A few minutes later David lies down on a colorful blanket. It's just too warm to cuddle today. The two have chosen a wonderful place on the beach.

A light wind blows over the white bodies of David and Dennis. The sun is shining.

After this short break both continue.

"Hasta luego." That means: "See you soon." Well then, Hasta luego, Spain.

Portugal

"Bom dia." A little girl with a strange costume greets in a friendly way. She wears a scarf around her head and around her neck. A beautiful floral pattern and embroidery are on her skirt.

Before the little David asks, Dennis already answers: "Bom dia" means "hello" in Portuguese, because we are in Portugal at the moment."

David grins. "I thought so." He approaches the little girl. "What's your name?"

The girl finds the two cats very likeable. "Elena, my name is Elena." She strokes David and Dennis. That flatters the two cats very much. Familiarly, they sit down next to Elena. David notes that the little girl is very shy.

He tries to distract her a little. "Can you tell us something about your country?"

"If you want, we'll take the yellow tram and I'll show you the city." Elena is helpful and feels very comfortable around David and Dennis.

"Hey, that's funny!" David likes this ancient tram.

"This is a good way to discover the city. It is tram number 28. It is also called Elétrico. Driving with this tram you can see the most beautiful squares and streets of Lisbon."

"Oh, see the beautiful fountain?" Dennis is enthusiastic about a place that is also called Rossio.

A little later they come to a place with a high tower. "Oh, I know what that is!" Dennis exclaims happily. "That's the Torre de Belém."

"Yes, that's right", Elena thinks it's great that he knows that.

The little David is proud of his clever brother. "Great, my brother knows a lot."

Elena wants to take a break and sits on a bench by the sea. She has a beautiful view of Lisbon's most famous landmark. "Do you know how high this tower is?"

Dennis continues to talk happily. "The top is 35 meter high, the exposed floor of the tower is an observation deck. In 1515 the Torre de Belém was commissioned by the Portuguese King Manuel I. As a symbol of protection for sailors, this tower looks out over the sea. On the north side is a rhino head."

"Sailors, yeah, that sounds exciting." The adventurous David would love to be a pirate himself.

Elena means: "Come on, let's go to the observation deck."

"No, I don't feel like walking again?" David yawns. He thinks it's stupid to walk so many stairs.

"We can also just sit on the bench, no problem." Elena would like to tell more about her country. David and Dennis listen attentively. "Portugal is located in Europe. Our country borders the Atlantic Ocean to the west and south, and Spain to the east and north. Portugal also includes the islands of the Azores and Madeira. The island of Madeira is called the flower island because beautiful flowers grow there. Funchal is the capital there."

"Hm, that all sounds very nice", but David only has one thing in mind: Food! "What do you eat in Portugal? Hope no cheese!"

Dennis has to smile because he knows his brother very well.

Elena wants Dennis to answer that. She looks at him questioningly: "Do you know that?"

"Yes, of course", nods Dennis, "bacalhau, for example. That's a salted and dried cod."

"That's right", smiles Elena, "but there are also dishes with other fish, vegetables, meat, rice and beans."

"Great, let's have fish then." David tastes one bite after the other with relish. "Fed up!", he announces and rubs his tummy with joy.

"I'm glad you enjoyed it." Elena looks at the clock and realizes with horror that it is getting late. "Oh, I have to go home now. It was nice to meet you both. Até logo. That means goodbye in Portuguese."

"Até logo, Elena."

David and Dennis enjoy the Portuguese sun a little longer and then continue on their journey of discovery.

Italy

Now we come to Italy. The sun always shines here.

"Why is this tower leaning so crooked? Doesn't anyone fall down?" David stands very amazed in front of this building.

"We are in Piazza dei Miracoli and we are facing an iconic symbol of the city, the Bell Tower (nicknamed: The Leaning Tower of Pisa)." Dennis also takes a closer look at the building and is fascinated.

"Do you think nobody really falls down there?" David asks again.

"No, but it's really amazing", says Dennis and continues: "Pisa is a world-famous city on the banks of the Arno River."

"Is Pisa the capital of Italy?", asks David curiously.

"No, the capital is Rome. If you want, we can go to Rome now", Dennis suggests to his brother.

"Yes of course. How do we get there?" David takes a quick look around. Most people drive here by car or moped. "Hey, a moped like that would be great." That would please the little joker.

A friendly boy has been listening to the two cats and offers to help. Willing to help, he takes both to Rome. Suddenly they stop in front of a huge building.

"Wow, that's a powerful house. Who lives here?" David is very impressed by that.

"This is where the Pope lives", Dennis explains affectionately.

"The pope?" David looks at his brother in surprise and frowns.

"Yes, he is the head of the Catholic Church", Dennis knows. "We are in St. Peter's Square in Rome, but the Pope has his own state, the Vatican, and in the center is a huge obelisk. This is a sign of the Christians. Many believers from all over the world meet here. For example, at Easter and Christmas. That all looks good, doesn't it?"

David is completely thrilled. "And so many people come here?"

Dennis nods. "Yes, they all pray together, it doesn't matter where they come from."

The little David becomes all calm and in awe. "That's wonderful." But even in this holy place he feels hungry.

"What is the Pope eating?", asks David curiously.

"Unfortunately, I don't know", answers Dennis. "But in Italy people like to eat pasta or pizza."

"Hmm, that sounds good. Where can you eat something here?" David looks around for a suitable location.

David and Dennis continue down the street. "There must be a Ristorante somewhere, that's what restaurants in Italy are called."

Then David discovers a sign that says "Ristorante".

"Ah, there is one." David happily hurries to the kitchen door, because he finds this door everywhere. His fine sense of smell always leads him in the right direction.

"Hm delicious. There is tomato sauce for the pasta." David licks the tomato sauce off the plate with relish. The red sauce settles in his whiskers. He rubs his face with his paws several times. This is a good sign that he liked it.

Dennis enjoys when his brother is so happy and he licks a piece of pizza with pineapple and ham.

After half an hour, the two cats sit down in the Italian sun.

Once again, they clean themselves thoroughly and take a nap in the afternoon.

"Arrivederci Italia."

"Goodbye Italy."

Greece

We are in a country with a lot of culture. The capital of Greece is Athens.

"Wow, is that a beautiful place!" David looks in amazement at the hill in front of him.

"This is the Acropolis, the symbol of the country and it means: The sublime." Dennis points to the many large pillars that belong to the Acropolis. The Acropolis was a fortress."

"The Olympics also have their origins in Greece. Nowadays athletes from all over the world meet every four years for the Olympic Games. Each time the Olympics take place in a different country."

David is impressed. "Great, just great."

The two cats walk through the capital Athens. How could it be any different. A few meters further, David stops in front of a Greek restaurant.

"Oh, what is the name of the national dish of Greece?", he asks in anticipation.

"For example, gyros. This is meat with hot spices." Dennis looks at the big skewer. "There's a lot of meat stacked there. This is eaten with tsatsiki, a yoghurt with garlic, cucumber and olive oil."

"Phew, that smells strong. Is that garlic?" David points to the many tubers hanging behind the counter.

"Yes, those are the garlic cloves. It smells a bit, but it's also healthy." Dennis knows that from home, where the cat mom sometimes cooks with garlic.

"And what else do the Greeks eat?"

"Moussaka. This is a casserole with fried potato slices, minced meat, olive oil, fried eggplant. Everything is gratinated with a béchamel sauce", reports Dennis.

David shows a lot of interest. "Is Greece a big country?"

"Yes, Greece also consists of many islands. The largest and most famous islands are for example Samos, Rhodes, Corfu and Crete. They are in the Aegean and Ionian Seas", says Dennis.

And David would like to visit these islands. "Can we go there?"

"We're happy to do that. There are ships down there. With them you can go to one of the islands. Would you like to see the island of Corfu?"

"Yes, of course." David immediately goes on a ship that takes him to this island. "Great view and the many mountains, great."

When the two cats go ashore, they look for a cozy spot and enjoy the view of the sea.

They sit next to a white house with a blue roof. This is typical for Greece.

"Come on, let's rest a little in the shade. The sun is pretty strong", suggests Dennis happily.

David immediately agrees to this. An afternoon nap is always good. Before the two reach their shady spot, their way is blocked by many sheep and goats.

"Oh no, people!" But before David can say anything else, he pricks up his ears. "Do you hear that?"

Dennis also listens to the sounds. "It's coming from the port, sounds like a bouzouki."

"Bouzouki?" The little David looks at his brother in surprise. "What is this again?"

"The bouzouki is a pear-shaped instrument. They used to make this out of a piece of wood, but now they make it out of shavings. The bouzouki is often played in folk dances, such as the sirtaki", reports Dennis.

"Sirtaki? What do you do with Sirtaki?"

"As people dance in a row, the dancers put their arms on the neighbor's shoulders."

David grins and secretly imagines himself dancing in a row like this. Must be fun.

After a short rest, David and Dennis move to the next country.

South Africa

"Phew, it's hot here." David wipes the beads of sweat from his forehead.

Dennis is also sweating. "Yes, it's always so warm here."

"Where are we?", asks David curiously.

"We are in South Africa. This is a country that is also called rainbow country."

"Why?"

"Because there are people with different skin colors here", Dennis replies.

"Goeiemiddag", a small, dark-skinned boy greets.

David doesn't have to guess long: "Goeiemiddag means hello?"

And Dennis nods. "Yes, that's right."

The little David sees a crowd of people passing him. "Where are all the people going?"

"They probably all go towards Table Mountain. Known as the landmark of Cape Town, South Africa, it encompasses 6000 hectares of cliffs and streams."

"We're in Cape Town right now?", asks David.

"Exactly. Cape Town is the second largest city in South Africa after Johannesburg. But the capital of the country is Pretoria. Cape Town was named after the Cape of Good Hope. This is about 45 kilometers south-east of Cape Town and was a great danger for sailors as the way across the sea was very turbulent."

How good that Dennis has researched everything so well.

David can't take his eyes off this mountain. "That looks great, this natural wonder."

Then he discovers a bench. "Let's go", and the little joker sits on his tender backside. "I need to catch my breath. Oh, that's good."

After a short moment of rest, the inquisitive David wants to find out more. "What else can you see here?"

Dennis thinks for a moment. "The Kruger National Park for example. It is the largest park and the country is home to many large animal species such as lion, leopard, buffalo, elephant and rhino."

"Oh great. Lions like us!" David winks at his brother.

Dennis is happy to continue reporting about the country: "South Africa is located at the southern tip of Africa. It borders the Indian Ocean and the Atlantic Ocean to the west. To the north are the neighboring countries of Namibia, Botswana and Zimbabwe, to the northeast is Mozambique and to the east is Swaziland."

"Aha." Now that's enough information for David. And how could it be otherwise, the next question is: "What do people in South Africa eat?"

"Here they eat ostrich meat, chicken legs, corn balls, potatoes, salads. Mostly lamb and beef. Herbs and spices are used liberally, for example coriander, cardamom, cloves, cinnamon, ginger and chilli", explains Dennis and grins because his beloved brother can't wait to eat.

"Ooh, the lamb sounds good", David thinks and he already has a piece of meat in his mouth.

Dennis likes to live healthy and would like to eat a salad with it.

"Smack! smack!" The two cats feel completely satisfied.

A well-deserved nap after dinner and then they continue with the discovery tour through the world.

India

We are in a far country with a lot of life. A maharaja ruled here. Today, many people from different parts of the world live in India. The landmark is the Taj Mahal.

"That's a very nice white house." David takes a closer look at the pillars of the building.

"Yes, it is the Taj Mahal." The beautiful building shines in the sun. "It was built by a maharajah."

David and Dennis stand fascinated in front of this big house.

"A maharajah?", asks David. "Who is that?"

"A maharaja is a former ruler of the country. It's like a king." Dennis continues: "He built this Taj Mahal out of love for a woman. This house is also a symbol of love."

"That's pretty impressive." David sits on a bench in front of the building. "Looks great."

Lots of people visit this place and the two cats stay there for quite a while too.

After an hour, David wants to know: "Do you know the national dish of India?"

"The national dish is called thali and consists mainly of rice. It is mixed with vegetables and fruits. The Indian dishes also have a lot of spices to make the dishes tasty, but sometimes they are quite spicy." Dennis takes a few steps. "Come on, let's go further, because in the markets you can buy all kinds of spices."

The Taj Mahal is located in Agra. The markets are far away.

"How are we supposed to get there?"

Than they see a rickshaw, a bicycle is turned into a car. There is one wheel in the front and two wheels in the back. They already borrow a rickshaw.

When they arrive at the market, the two cats continue to look around. David finds it all very exciting. "It's exciting here. People haggle for money. Are there no fixed prices?"

"No, people act. That's fun for most people", explains Dennis. "There is really a lot to see. For example, the spices like cardamom, cumin, turmeric and coriander."

"But what do people in this country do when they're not at the market?", asks the little David curiously.

"They pray in the country's mosques. Many people are Hindus, a well-known religious group." Dennis heard that somewhere.

Everything sounds very interesting. David sits on a wall. "Now I need a break, so many new impressions, it makes me tired."

And Dennis nods. "Yes, we'll take an afternoon nap then."

"Oh, before I forget, what is the name of the capital of India?" David blinks at his brother with small eyes.

"The capital is New Delhi. But we're not going there anymore." Dennis lies down next to his brother. Then they move on in thought.

"Bye India."

China

David stands in amazement in front of these huge walls: "What is that? That looks huge."

"Yes, this is the symbol of China. The Great Wall of China. Gigantic, isn't it?" Dennis is also very impressed.

"Phew, that's a long wall. You have to walk a lot. It's guaranteed to make you hungry." And the little David has only one thought: "What do the Chinese eat?"

"The Chinese usually eat rice and vegetables from the wok." Dennis heard that when two tourists were talking.

"Wok? What's that again?" David would like to know.

"The wok looks a bit like a frying pan, but it's bigger and taller", explains Dennis.

"Ah, but just rice and veggies? Is there any meat?" David is just a gourmet.

"The Chinese also like to eat Beijing duck", Dennis adds: "Beijing is the capital of China."

"Duck is good. It must taste delicious. But how do we get to the city now?"

"With a rickshaw", Dennis replies and points to the bicycles on the side of the road. "Well, I think a rickshaw is a vehicle like in India, but that was more of a car", David thinks.

"Yes, that's right. Here a rickshaw looks more like a rider and a human is pedaling." Dennis points to a bicycle approaching them.

The two jump into the rickshaw and come into town. There they sit comfortably in a restaurant and enjoy a delicious Beijiing duck.

"Where are we going now?"

"We could still go to Hong Kong." Dennis is happy to accompany his brother, because he also enjoys traveling.

"Hong Kong?", asks the enterprising David. "What can you see there?"

"Hong Kong is also a big city. The climate is tropical humid, so we will sweat a lot there." But that doesn't matter, because David would like to get to know the country.

"All right then. Hong Kong is also called the fragrant port", explains Dennis.

"Great, let's go."

"There is the so-called Victoria Tower, which is a lookout tower over the city", and Dennis knows more: "Victoria Peak is the most famous mountain in Hong Kong. The Chinese call this Tai Ping Shan, which means: Mountain of Great Peace."

"Great." But now the little David is getting tired. Happy and full, the two lie down in the midday sun and dream of their next travel destination.

Australia

Australia is a huge country on the Pacific Ocean. All the animals of this continent are big and strong, like the kangaroo or the koala bear. The secret capital is Sydney.

"Phew, it's pretty hot here." David stands on a large bridge in Sydney Harbour.

"Many believe that Sydney is the capital of Australia, but that's not true", Dennis says thoughtfully. "Canberra is the capital."

And David marvels. "There's a gigantic building over there."

"Yes, this is the Sydney Opera House, a landmark of the country", knows Dennis.

"It looks like a rising shell. And look, so many ships enter the port. Wow, great." Curious, David moves on. He notices that there are many cars driving here.

"It`s very busy here." David stands on the street and watches the hustle and bustle.

"That's right. Come on, let's go to a quieter place." Dennis leads his brother into a green landscape called the jungle.

"Here is the Australian jungle. There are many wild animals living and there are quite a few tripping hazards for people and animals." Dennis looks at the hanging bridge in front of them.

The little David is not comfortable with this rocking thing. "I'm not going there." Actually, he is not afraid, but now he takes a few steps back. "This is too dangerous."

"I'm not comfortable with it either." Dennis is careful too. The two cats prefer to make their way into town.

They pass a restaurant. Of course, David has only one thought: "What's on the menu?"

"The Australians like to eat ostrich steak."

David frowns. "What does an ostrich look like?"

Dennis describes it like this: "An ostrich is large, has long legs, thick plumage and a pointed beak."

And David listens to his brother very attentively.

This animal probably poke everywhere with the beak. "No, I do not like it. Let's move on. Maybe there is something else to eat? What do you mean?"

Dennis agrees and goes on to say: "People like to meet for a barbecue. They eat grilled meat and vegetables. That is delicious."

He sees another delicacy in a shop window. A pie.

"This is the pavlova cake. This dish is also popular in Australia."

David and Dennis sit down on a bench again.

They take a little break and Dennis continues: "A landmark of the country or the continent is the Great Barrier Reef. It was discovered by a British explorer in 1770. His name is James Cook."

David listens attentively and Dennis continues to tell: "The Great Barrier Reef is located in northeastern Australia on the east coast and is the largest coral reef. With a boat you can observe the underwater world. There are many plants and animals."

"That is interesting. Are we going there?"

On the one hand, the little David is curious and wants to know everything, on the other hand, he would like to take another break because it's so hot.

"Let's move on after the break", his brother asks, "there are still so many beautiful places to see."

That's fine with David and so they travel to the next country in their minds.

"Bye Australia."

New Zealand

"Böh, böh", blocks a sheep and pushes David. He is slightly angry. "Hey, what are you doing? Why are you pushing me? That`s the last straw!"

But the sheep only shouts: "Böh!"

David can't believe it. "Where did we end up here?"

"We are in New Zealand", replies Dennis.

"New Zealand? Where is that?", the little David wants to know.

"New Zealand is an island country in the southern Pacific Ocean and consists of a northern and a southern island and many smaller islands", reports Dennis and continues: "The country is about 2000 kilometers east of Australia. After Australia, New Zealand is the second largest producer of wool. There are many millions of sheep living in New Zealand."

David is still angry. "Great, but if there are so many of them, then no one needs to bump into me." Than he runs through the legs of the sheep in a flash and sits down in a safe place at the end of the pasture. "Phew, hopefully no one pushes here."

And David turns around and looks for a brother. "Come on, let's go somewhere else."

The two cats continue walking and pass a place where many people are cheering loudly.

"What are these people playing?" David looks questioningly at the crowd.

"Rugby", replies Dennis. "Rugby is similar to football here. It's a popular sport in New Zealand."

"Ah, I also like to play soccer." But before David wants to go on a tour of discovery, he asks a very specific question: "What do people eat in New Zealand?"

"New Zealanders like to eat meat, poultry, vegetables, desserts, fish and chips, and roast lamb", Dennis knows.

"Aha." Then David discovers a little boy who is wearing something strange. This so-called Maori kilt consists of flax leaves. It is worn by Maori men and women.

David is just examining the boy.

"This is a Maori boy", Dennis knows and his brother frowns. "Maori?"

Suddenly the boy nudges David´s nose.

"Hey what are you doing?"

This is quite normal for the little boy, because the Maoris are the indigenous people of New Zealand and that's how they greet each other.

"Kia ora", greets the little Maori boy and Dennis smiles. "Kia ora means hello in the Maori language."

David also nudges the little boy's nose in a friendly manner and he enjoys it a lot. But the curious David wants to know more about the country and so Dennis starts with the information. "The symbol of New Zealand is the kiwi."

David shouts proudly: "Great, I know that, that's a fruit."

"Yes, too, but in New Zealand that's a bird. This flightless bird is the heraldic animal of New Zealand. It is under nature protection."

Now the little David is horrified. "How the bird can't fly?" A bird that can't fly, no, David doesn't understand that. That's very unusual.

"Yes, that's the way it is. I don't know why that is either." Dennis shrugs and continues: "Wellington is the capital of New Zealand. It is the second largest city in this country after Auckland. It is located on the southern tip of the North Island."

David continues to listen intently.

"Then there is another national park, Tongariro National Park. This is located in the center of the North Island and is the fourth oldest national park in the world."

"So, so", it comes hesitantly from David´s mouth.

Then the two cats are on their way to Hokitika. There is a large jade factory there.

Dennis is enthusiastic about the many precious stones. "That's nice! We could buy a jade necklace for our mom."

And David immediately agrees: "That's a great idea."

After they bought the present for their mom, David realizes something very important. "I absolutely have to eat a little bit!"

He discovers a delicious candy called Hokey Pokey. David thinks that's funny. "What is it?"

"Hokey Pokey is vanilla ice cream with toffees. But we should have a main meal first", says Dennis.

"Sure, let's have the roast lamb", means David and the two of them eat with relish.

After the delicious meal, David and Dennis say goodbye to New Zealand.

Samoa

"Tálofa." A little girl with a white blouse and a black skirt meets the two cats.

"Tálofa", Dennis replies politely. "That means hello?", David guesses and his brother nods with a smile.

The little girl is in a good mood and caresses the two. "What are you doing here?"

"We go on a journey of discovery through the world. Where are we?" David would like to know.

"You are in Samoa", the girl replies and tells more about her country. "Samoa is located in the southwest Pacific. The largest islands are Savaii and Upolu. But there are also many uninhabited islands".

"Ah, nice, nice", nods David, "and what are you doing here?"

"I go to school, study hard and at lunchtime I help my mum with the dishes", the little one replies a little shyly.

"That is very exemplary." Dennis is happy to see such a nice girl.

"What's your name?", David asks curiously.

"My name is Maria", she replies. "My grandmother's name is Maria and she comes from Germany."

Dennis smiles. "Maria is a beautiful name."

And the little David thinks so too.

Now they are standing in front of a large church.

"Are you going in here?" David asks.

"Yes, every Sunday the whole family goes to church. We are all Catholic, like most people in Samoa. This is the Mulivai Cathedral, the landmark of Apia."

Before asking a question, Maria gives the answer: "Apia is the capital of Samoa" and continues: "You can tell from Samoa's coat of arms that we are so religious in Samoa. It says "Founded on God" on it." She is proud of her country and loves living in Samoa.

"And what else is there to report about Samoa?" asks David expectantly.

Maria doesn't think twice. "Samoa is an island country. Samoa used to be part of New Zealand. But in 1962 it gained independence. We speak Samoan and English here. Many cruise ships dock here and bring a lot of tourists into the country. Most people want to hike, dive or sail."

After a few minutes, the three are in front of the school building.

"Now I have to learn something." Maria would have liked to spend more time with the two cats, but no pain, no gain.

"Tófá", she says politely. That means goodbye in Samoan.

David and Dennis say goodbye and wave to Maria.

"A very nice girl", Dennis raves.

"Yes, she is super nice and she told us so much about Samoa." David looks questioningly at his brother. "Do you also know anything else about the country?"

"Yes, there is something else to be said about this independence. The country was then called Western Samoa. There is also an eastern part of Samoa called American Samoa."

David smiles mischievously. "You are always so smart."

"Thank you very much", laughs Dennis, and knows even more: "The larger islands are of volcanic origin. The small islands are formed from coral reefs."

"Interesting." David's thirst for knowledge has now been quenched. He sets out to find a tasty meal. It has to be. What else should he ask at this point? "What do they eat in Samoa?"

"People like to eat plantains and breadfruit."

David doesn't seem to like that and Dennis continues to report. "Don't worry, there are other specialties too. For example: Oka. There are pieces of fish or vegetables marinated in coconut cream."

After tasting this delicacy, the two find a nice place under a tree.

Then David and Dennis are already dreaming of their next adventure destination.

"Well then, Tófá, Samoa."

Mexico

"Hola muchachos." A good-humored gentleman in a colorful coat walks through the streets of Mexico City, the country's capital.

"Hola", replies David cheerfully. "Hola means hello again, right?", he looks at his brother mischievously.

"Something like that", answers Dennis, "hola means hello. In Spanish, people greet each other during the day with buenas tardes."

"Alright, but it doesn't matter, look at those bold colors on that coat!" David is completely fascinated by this play of colors. Only he realizes that the coat doesn't look anything like the coat his mum wears at home.

Dennis nods. "Of course, this coat that the man is wearing is also called a poncho. In the past, this coat was made from a piece of cloth. A slit was made in the middle so you could pull this coat over your head. And this coat or poncho just lies on your shoulders."

"Great", David thinks and discovers something else unusual that the man is wearing. "And what's on his head?"

"That's a sombrero. This hat is made of straw or felt and has a wide brim. In the past, field workers wore a hat like this to protect themselves from the sun."

"Sure, this hat is also very big", David grins and he is once again amazed at how educated his brother is.

Suddenly there is music.

"Oh, what strange thing is that man holding?"

"It's a pan flute", says Dennis. "The pan flute consists of a series of tubes that can be made of wood or bamboo. This allows you to produce very high tones."

"That sounds good", but David is just wondering which country they are actually in.

"We're in Mexico", Dennis knows. "This country borders on the United States of America (USA), on the Pacific Ocean, Guatemala, Belize and the Caribbean Sea, on the east on the Gulf of Mexico. Mexico is the fifth largest country in the American double continent, North and South America."

The little David is curious again: "And do they speak Spanish here?"

"Yes, the Spaniards came to this country many centuries ago. The country was originally home to the Mayans. There is also the famous Mayan calendar. Mayan writing consists only of symbols in images. The Maya lived in southern and southeastern Mexico, on the Yucatán Peninsula. There is a Mayan city that is a landmark in Mexico. There are the pyramids of Chichén Itzá and they are located in the north of the peninsula. Pyramids are the symbol of Mexico."

"Anything you don't already know", smiles David. But he is glad that his brother gives him so much information.

In the capital of Mexico, Mexico City, David notices a huge building.

"Look over there! That's a huge tower!" He points to the so-called skyscraper.

"This is the Torre latinoamericana. It has 45 floors and is 182 meters high."

And David amazed: "Oh my goodness, that's high!"

But the little David is interested in something completely different. "Well, I'd be hungry for something hearty. Is there such a thing in Mexico?"

Dennis thinks for a moment: "As far as I know, people like to eat tacos here. These are small tortillas, kind of like pancakes. There are different fillings and sauces, like the salsa mexicana."

"Great, then let's try it!" David buys tacos with gyros filling. "Hm delicious!"

After this small refreshment they continue to the next country.

"Hasta luego. Bye Mexico."

Brazil

David covers his ears. "Where's that noise coming from?"

The loud clatter of drums resounds through the streets and now he has to stand in a crowd: "I want out of here!"

Dennis agrees. "It's all colorful and glitters a lot, but it's also super loud."

The two cats try to get to the other side of the street. This is not so easy.

An elderly lady takes the two on her shoulders. She wears a wide skirt and a turban-like headgear.

David is a bit skeptical at first, but he also enjoys the view from the lady's shoulders. He likes being carried. "That's a wonderful observation position."

The lady drops David and Dennis across the street. "Well, that's done!"

She tenderly strokes the backs of the two cats. She feels the velvety soft fur and immediately takes them both to her heart.

David and Dennis say thank you politely. "That's very kind of you, thank you."

"You're nice", says David, "what's your name?"

The older lady winks at him. "I am Julia."

And David notices that she is wearing something strange.

She senses his thoughts and answers him. "This is the national costume of Brazil."

"Ah, so we're in Brazil", he states. "Is it always this loud in here?"

"Yes, Brazilians are always in a good mood, dancing and singing. But most of all at carnival time, when the students of all the samba schools dance in their wonderful costumes. You can show them off in a parade", Julia proudly reports.

Dennis asks a little shyly: "Can you tell us more about your country?"

"Yes, with pleasure", Julia replies. "Come on, let's go to the beach, we'll have a little more peace there."

Arriving at the beach, the three find a beautiful picture of blue water, a high mountain and a white sand beach. David and Dennis agree: "It's great here."

Julia is happy that the two are enjoying the panorama. "That is the Copacabana, a sandy beach about 4 kilometers long. We are located in the city of Rio de Janeiro, the second largest city in Brazil. For almost 200 years, Rio de Janeiro was the capital, but since 1960, Brasilia has been the country's capital."

Julia continues: "The landmarks of Rio de Janeiro are the Sugar Loaf, the statue of Christ on the top of Corcovado and the beach here."

"Great!" David enthuses and asks mischievously: "Is the sugar loaf made of sugar too?"

"No, no", Julia laughs, "the sugar loaf is 395 meters high and a steep bell-shaped mountain on the Urca peninsula."

David and Dennis look at the huge statue. And Julia goes on to explain: "Yes, that's impressive. This is Cristo Redentor, which means Christ the Redeemer. The statue of Christ stands on 8 meter high base. Measured from left to right, the arms are 28 meters wide. The statue weighs 1145 tons and looks straight at Sugarloaf Mountain."

This very interesting and David wants to know more: "And where exactly is Brazil located?"

Julia likes to continue playing the tour guide. "Brazil is located in South America and borders on Argentina, Uruguay, Paraguay, Bolivia, Peru, French Guiano, Suriname, Guyana, Venezuela and Colombia."

"Wow, that's a lot of states", the little David marvels.

"Brazil is also a huge country, the fifth largest country in the world. More than 200 million people love it here", reports Julia and tells us even more: "The Amazon is the most important river. It is about 300 kilometers south of the equator. It is shaped by the tropical rain forests."

"Tropics, oh dear", that reminds David that the tropical climate is very humid. "No thanks. That's too wet for me."

A little girl approaches the three of them.

"Bom dia."

Julia knows the little one and introduces her. "This is Larissa, my little granddaughter."

"Bom dia, isn't that portuguese?" He's heard that before in Portugal.

"That's right", explains Julia, "Portuguese is the national language in Brazil."

A slight growl can be heard from David's stomach. "What delicacies can you eat in Brazil?"

Julia laughs. "Oh, that's difficult. There are so many immigrants here and everyone brought something with them. I can't name a real national dish. But people like to eat feijoada, which is a bean stew."

David looks at his brother: "Oh, beans! You know, every bean makes a sound! I think we better leave that alone."

Julia has to smile, but she also has another dish to offer. "There is also the bacalhau, the fish like in Portugal. Or fruits like mangoes, figs, papayas, guavas, oranges, passion fruit, pears and pineapples."

David and Dennis choose the fish. That is healthy.

After dinner they take another nap. That feels good.

They say goodbye to Julia and Larissa.

"Adeus, bye, Brazil."

Fiji Islands

A wonderful scent of hibiscus blossoms fills the little noses of the two cats.

"Oh, that smells great." David and Dennis are absolutely thrilled.

A little girl takes a liking to the two cats and approaches them. "That smells really good, doesn't it?"

David would like to know her name.

"My name is Maria, I am a farmer's daughter." She immediately trusts David and Dennis, although she is actually quite shy.

"Where are we?"

"You are in Suva. This is the capital of the Fiji Islands on the island of Viti Levu", Maria reports proudly.

"Ah, right, right." David has noticed that people are very happy here. They dance and have fun.

Maria senses his thoughts. "Yes, we celebrate Hibiscus Festival for one week in August now."

Dennis is excited. "Very nice, you can feel the life energy and joy. Can you tell us more about your country?"

Maria loves doing that. "The Fiji Islands are north of New Zealand and east of Australia in the South Pacific. We have a coastline of about 1129 kilometers here. The region consists of 332 islands. 110 of them are inhabited. The main islands are Viti Levu and Vanua Levu. The highest mountain in our country is Tomanivi on the island of Viti Levu. It is 1324 meters high."

David finds that it has gotten very warm. "Phew, it's hot here."

Mary can only confirm that. "Yes, I can well imagine that you are warm. Here we have a tropical, hot and humid climate with temperatures ranging from 16 to 32 degrees Celsius. From November to April we have summer time and it rains a lot. Then there are always tropical storms, which are called cyclones. In the winter time, from May to October, the air is cooler."

They sit down in a shady corner at the side of the road. A new smell hits David's little snub nose.

"It smells like food!" He is wide awake immediately. His gaze falls on something green.

Maria gives him the answer without asking. "Here they cook on banana leaves."

"On banana leaves?" David and Dennis have never heard of that.

Maria is happy to explain: "It is a tradition on the Fiji Islands to cook in an earth oven. A fire is made in a sand hollow and a little sand is poured over it. The food is then placed in banana leaves and cooked for hours."

The little David is horrified. "For hours? Well, when should he eat?"

But Maria goes on to say: "A staple food is the taro root. There are also fresh fish, seafood, poultry, pork and beef. There is also duruka, which is a potato-like vegetable. It looks like cane."

An elderly gentleman sits down with the three. It is Maria's grandfather. He listened carefully to his granddaughter. And he also noticed that David was impatient.

"This is already done. It's beef. Try it", the older man asks the two cats and David already has a piece of cooked meat in his mouth.

Dennis likes it too.

The two cats look contentedly at the happy people at the hibiscus festival.

After a while they say goodbye.

"It's all nice here, but we're going on our world tour."

United States of America

This continent is divided into several states and in North and South America. For example, the Statue of Liberty in New York is a national landmark.

David stands on a bridge in New York City harbor and looks at a giant statue. "Wow, that woman is tall."

"This is Lady Liberty, the Statue of Liberty." Dennis is impressed too. "She is the symbol of freedom, independence and hope."

And David takes a closer look at this statue. "Why is the lady raising her arm so high and why is she carrying a torch?" He takes a huge pair of binoculars that are attached to the side of the road.

His brother is excited. "Yes, the torch means enlightenment."

Then David notices the many high-rise buildings in New York City. "These houses here are pretty big, they're almost hanging in the clouds."

Dennis is a good travel guide and so he continues to report about the country: "America is a so-called double continent."

"Double continent?", asks David and is amazed.

"There is North America and South America. North America is divided into many states such as California, Florida, Arizona, Texas, Nevada, Oklahoma and many more. The President of the country has his seat in

Washington. The so-called White House is his home. There is no single capital. Every state has one."

Dennis explains more: "In South America there are the so-called ABC countries. These are Argentina, Brazil and Chile. These three countries border each other."

"That all sounds interesting." David continues to listen to the words of his beloved brother: "There are so many beautiful cities in America. For example, on the west coast of the country are the cities of Los Angeles and San Francisco. Los Angeles comes from the Spanish: The angels. And in San Francisco you can walk on the Golden Gate Bridge. The bridge is located in San Francisco Bay."

Expectantly, David asks: "Are we going everywhere now?"

"No, we would be on the road too long because America is a big country. Maybe later."

Oh, David's stomach growls. "What do Americans eat?"

"Burgers and hot dogs", Dennis replies and also feels a little hungry.

"Burger? What is a burger made of?", David asks curiously.

And Dennis can help here too. "For example, a burger consists of ground beef, sesame bun, onions, lettuce and tomato ketchup. You can eat burgers with or without cheese. This is called fast food, i.e. a meal that is prepared quickly. In America you can eat burgers anywhere."

"And what is a hot dog? Hope people don't eat dogs?"
The little David looks horrified.

But Dennis can calm his brother down. "No, no, they don't eat dogs. That would be cruel. A hot dog is a boiled sausage sandwiched between a long bun. You eat mustard with it."

Suddenly, David discovers a fast food restaurant. "I would like to try a burger." He just can't make up his mind, there are too many varieties.

David takes a double burger and would like to eat another one. But this food is so much that he can no longer eat a second burger.

He strokes his well-filled stomach and lies down in the sun.

"Have you eaten anything?", David asks his brother.

"Yes, donuts. They are big and sweet."

After the sumptuous meal, the two cats lie down and dream of the next travel destination.

"Bye America. See you later. Maybe we'll come back again."

Canada

"Phew, the water is pounding against the rock." David and Dennis stand amazed in front of a gigantic spectacle of water.

The two agree: "It looks fantastic!"

The curious David wants to know where they are right now.

"We're at Niagara Falls in Canada", Dennis replies.

"Yes, that's right." A self-confident girl stands next to David and Dennis.

"Niagara Falls is located on the border between the Canadian province of Ontario and the American state of New York. That's great, isn't it?"

"Yes, of course." David looks at the girl. "But who are you?"

"I'm Olivia", the little girl replies.

David and Dennis think she is kind. "Nice to meet you, Olivia."

The little David is curious again. "Are you from this area?"

"No, I'm just on vacation here. My parents and I live in Ottawa, which is the capital of Canada." And she talks and talks: "Ottawa is located in the eastern part of the province of Ontario on the Ottawa River. This is on the border with the province of Quebec. Ottawa is the fourth largest city in Canada."

David and Dennis find it all very interesting.

"Can you tell us more about the country?"

Olivia is happy. "Oh yes, a lot. Canada is a North American country that lies between the Atlantic Ocean to the east and the Pacific Ocean to the west. In the north it extends to the Arctic Ocean. Canada is the second largest country in the world. About 12,000 years ago the Indians came into the country and settled it. Then came the English and French, so we speak English and French. It is said that Giovani Caboto, an Italian navigator, discovered the land."

The two cats listen carefully.

Olivia continues to tell. "There is so much to see here. For example, the Rocky Mountains, which are located in the western part of North America. Here is also the Yellowstone National Park. Established on March 1, 1872, it is the oldest national park in the world. The name was taken from the Yellowstone River, the main river in the park. There you will find many animals such as bison, grizzly bears and wolves."

Olivia notices that David and Dennis are not bored and continues to report. "Canada also has a lot of lake areas. 563 lakes are larger than 100 square kilometers."

David doesn't mean to be rude, but he's getting a little hungry.

And Dennis just wants to know the name of Canada's landmark.

"That's the maple leaf," Olivia replies. "The sugar maple is the most important tree in the country and is widespread. There's also a lot of maple syrup."

David listens up. "This has something to do with food."

And what question is he asking?

"What do you eat in Canada?"

Olivia doesn't need to think twice. "This varies by region. But I like to eat French fries, they often come with vinegar here."

David makes a face! "With vinegar?"

Olivia laughs. "Of course, you can also have ketchup."

David can smile again immediately. "Great, then I'll have fries with ketchup."

But Olivia offers even more: "There are other specialties, namely creamy clam chowder soup. It is made from diced potatoes and shrimp. Of course, there are also waffles with maple syrup."

Ah, Dennis doesn't say no. It is well known that he likes sweet foods.

After a short lunch break, David and Dennis have to continue their world tour. "Bye Canada. Canada is a very beautiful country."

Ireland

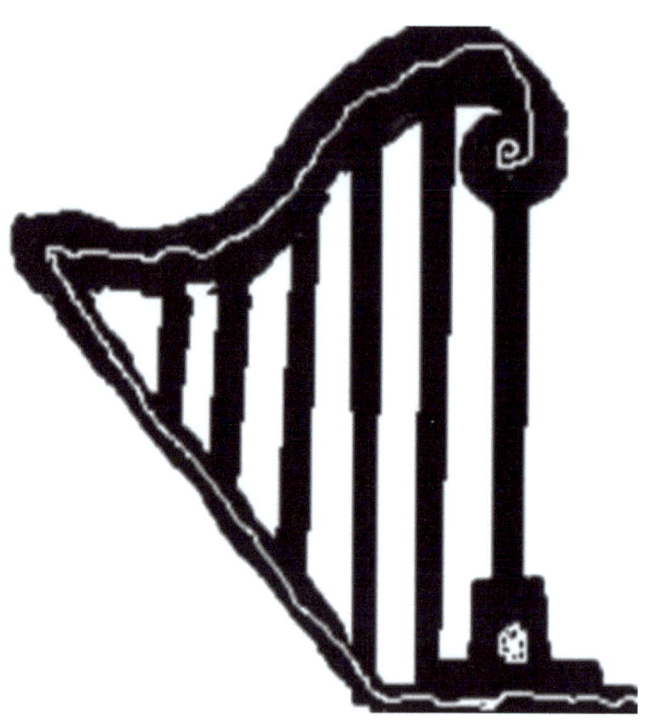

"Wow, that's great!" David exclaims with delight.

"This is Ireland! Rough cliffs, lonely sandy beaches, mystical places, lots of green land. That is why Ireland is also called the Emerald Isle." Dennis is also fascinated by this country.

It's quite windy here and so the two let the fresh wind blow around their noses.

Dennis can't stop raving about this beautiful country. "There are also many national parks and hills here. A 170-kilometer coastal road runs along the west coast. It's called the Ring of Kerry. You will also find tiny bays, small fishing villages and ruins from the Middle Ages."

David notices something. "Oh, there are sheep here too", he grins mischievously.

"Yes, Ireland has a lot to offer", says Dennis, listening to the music that reaches his ears.

"This is the sound of a harp", Dennis knows.

David also likes this music. "That sounds nice. Come on, let's take a closer look."

Curious, the two make their way to the next village.

A lady with long black hair plays the harp. Around her, many people are listening to this music.

"The harp is a symbol of Ireland", Dennis whispers.

His brother nods. This is followed by thunderous applause for the artist. She bows graciously to the audience.

"Dia duit", says a boy standing in front of the two cats. He wears a white shirt, black trousers and a colorfully embroidered waistcoat.

Dennis knows immediately what that means. "That means God with you and that's how people greet people here."

"We're about to dance an Irish folk dance. Are you looking at that?", the boy asks.

David and Dennis agree: "Sure, we'll do that."

Suddenly David notices that the girls also wear dirndls.

"Yes, that's right!" Dennis nods.

After the folk dance, the two cats move on to Dublin. This is the capital of Ireland. Dublin is on the east coast.

Of course, Dennis continues to play the guidebook: "There is a large zoo in Dublin. It is located in Phoenix Park and is a very popular attraction. After Vienna, London and Paris, it is the fourth-oldest zoo in the world."

Then Dennis thinks of something else: "Oh, I forgot. The coat of arms of the Republic of Ireland consists of a harp on a blue background. Yes, and the shamrock is the national symbol of Ireland."

"Super. Can you tell us more about this beautiful country?"

Dennis is very enthusiastic and continues to tell: "There is a lot to report, but one thing is still a nice tradition. St. Patrick's Day is celebrated on March 17th every year. The Irish commemorate a bishop who bore the name Patrick. He is the patron saint of Ireland."

But David's thirst for knowledge is slowly being quenched. He has to yawn. So much information makes him a little tired.

"Excuse me, but I have to yawn again."

But what would such a charming country be without a delicious meal? David asks his famous question: "What do people eat in Ireland?"

Dennis doesn't have to think long: "Irish stew. These are potatoes, onions, lamb, carrots, parsley and parsnips."

"Great, then let's eat that!"

After the meal David and Dennis clean up and look for a nice place to take a nap. The two make themselves comfortable on a bench.

In their dreams, they continue to travel.

David and Dennis agree: "Yes, bye Ireland. It's really very nice here."

Great Britain

This country is also called England. It's a country with a lot of history and it's represented by a queen. The symbol of the capital London is Big Ben.

"Where are we? The cars drive on the wrong side! Oops." A car almost hit little David. But his brother helps him and pulls him onto the nearest sidewalk.

Dennis is glad that nothing happened to his brother. "We are in the UK and cars drive on the left. So be careful, not like at home. In Germany, cars drive on the right."

Frightened but also grateful, David looks at his brother. "Thank you for being there for me."

Dennis smiles. "You are welcome. You are my brother and I love you with all my heart."

David smiles back. "I love you too."

He looks at a tall tower. "What is it?"

"This is Big Ben, a famous clock tower. Since 2012 it has been called Elizabeth Tower."

Dennis continues: "The Queen of England is called Elizabeth II. She celebrated her 60th anniversary of the throne in 2012 and Big Ben was renamed in her honor. Big Ben is part of the Palace of Westminster."

The two cats go on.

David can't get the queen out of his head. "Queen Elizabeth, where does she live?", he asks curiously.

"She lives sometimes in Buckingham Palace and sometimes in Windsor Castle, a family home. Buckingham Palace is located in London, the capital of Great Britain."

David stands in amazement in front of the palace. "Oh, but the lady has many rooms."

The next moment a black limousine drives by.

"That's the Queen!", Dennis exclaims enthusiastically.

"She's nice, she waves so nicely", David thinks, and he's happy about this friendly encounter.

David hears a few words that sound like five and tea. "What did the lady say?" Unfortunately he couldn't understand everything.

"Oh, the Queen's going to five o'clock tea for sure", Dennis explains.

"Why is she drinking tea at five o'clock?"

"It's a tradition in Great Britain. It's not just the queen who does that. They drink tea and eat sandwiches. These are small bites."

Food is always good, David thinks, and would like to know what these sandwiches are made of.

Dennis is happy to explain: "The appetizers consist of bread, meat, salad and sauce. Sandwiches are sandwiches. But there are also scones that are served with whipped cream and jam."

"Hmm, that sounds delicious. Would the Queen invite us to five o'clock tea?", asks David mischievously.

Dennis shrugs. "I don't know, but the lady doesn't even know us."

"And what else do they eat in Great Britain?" David is very interested in the country and its people.

"People like to eat fish and chips. This is a fish fillet fried in batter, served with thick slices of potato." Dennis is very fond of fish.

And the little gourmet David would like to know if there is also a dessert.

Sweet Dennis can also provide information on this: "Yorkshire pudding is a well-known English pastry. This pancake batter consists of milk, flour, eggs, fat, salt, pepper, parsley and nutmeg. Jam is served with it."

"That must taste good too." But today David can't try everything.

The two cats are walking down a long street in front of Buckingham Palace.

"How about a little rest? We've walked so much. There are many beautiful trees along this road, you can definitely take a rest there."

David immediately agrees to a break.

In their dreams, the two continue to travel.

Where? You'll find out in the next story.

"Bye bye Great Britain."

Scotland

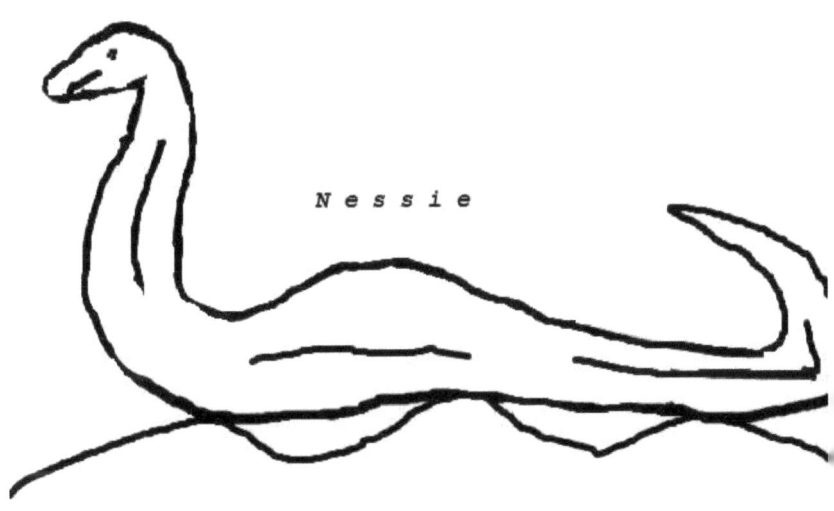

Nessie

"Oh, the man is wearing a skirt! Only girls and women do that, right?" David looks at the gentleman standing in front of him several times.

Well, the man is wearing a plaid skirt and matching stockings. Little David thinks that's strange.

Dennis smiles: "Yes, that's right, usually only girls and women wear skirts. But we are in Scotland and here men also wear a so-called kilt."

David frowns: "A kilt? Oops."

His brother has to smile. "Yes, a kilt is a knee-length men's skirt."

The man feels he is being watched and turns around. "Hello, I am John."

"Hello, Mr. John", Dennis replies.

"Where are you from?" asks the friendly gentleman.

"We're from Germany", says Dennis, looking a little shy.

David can't get this man's skirt out of his head. "Why are you wearing the skirt? You're not a girl."

John smiles. "No, but what your brother said is true, it's a tradition here in Scotland."

He points to a whistle with long reeds. "And that's a bagpipe." He proudly carries this so-called bagpipe in his arm.

Now John begins to play the bagpipe. The shrill noise is too loud for David and he covers his ears. "Great welcome! It could be a little quieter."

John immediately stops playing and prefers to talk about his home country. "Scotland is part of Great Britain, the United Kingdom and Northern Ireland. The capital is Edinburgh and has two different sides. On the one hand, Edinburgh is the traditional Old Town with narrow streets, the famous Royal Mile and centuries-old buildings. The second part is Edinburgh's New Town. Here is the modern district with a lot of business."

John is happy to continue: "There is a fiery red landmark in the city. It is the Forth Bridge with a length of 2.7 kilometers. This bridge spans the Firth of Forth. It connects Edinburgh with the neighboring region of Kingdom of Fife and has been a UNESCO World Heritage Site since 2015."

David and Dennis listen carefully to John. He speaks with a Scottish accent.

John smiles: "We speak mostly English but also Scottish Gaelic, some of us speak Scots. But that's not many anymore."

And he continues to report on his country: "Scotland is located in the northern third of Great Britain and has an area of 78,772 square kilometers. It is divided into the Highlands, Central Lowlands and Southern Uplands. The highest mountain in Scotland is Ben Nevis near Fort William."

Dennis thinks. "Highlands, I've heard that before. That's the Scottish Highlands, isn't it?"

John enjoys Dennis' knowledge. "Yes, that is correct. The Highlands are in north-west Scotland. There are many lakes here and some deeply cut sea arms, which are called holes. Like Loch Ness for example."

"Loch Ness?" The two cats have to laugh a little. That sounds funny.

"Yes, that's right. There's even a sea monster called Nessie", John says.

"Nessie!" shouts David. "That sounds like a chocolate ad."

Dennis shakes his head. "You only think about food again."

His brother nods and continues listening to what John has to say. "It is said that there have been people who have seen this monster for centuries. Therefore, Loch Ness is a tourist attraction."

It all sounds very interesting what John says. "I have something to say about the Highlands. The Highland Games take place at up to 100 locations in Scotland from May to October. These are traditional sporting competitions, such as throwing logs. The thrower holds the log vertically in front of his body, runs up and throws the log away. It shouldn't tip over."

"Aha." But David has heard enough now and his stomach is making noises. He asks the question again: "What do you eat in Scotland?"

John doesn't think twice. "Haggis."

David looks at John. "Haggis? What is it?"

"This is the national dish of Scotland and a specialty made from sheep's stomach." John can't continue because he sees the horrified faces of David and Dennis.

The two cats agree: "Ooh, that's disgusting. No, thanks."

John offers them a pastry called shortbread.

But the two refuse. We have to move on anyway. "Slàn. That means goodbye in Gaelic."

"So then, slàn Scotland."

Sweden

"Oh dear, what is that?", exclaims David as he hikes through one of Sweden's many national parks.

"Pssst, that's a moose." Dennis gently places the right paw on his brother's little mouth.

But David wants to know more. "A moose! Wow! But he has a mighty thing on his head."

"Yes, that's an antler. The males of the elk carry this", explains Dennis and continues: "The maximum width of an antler is 2 meters. The antlers are shed every year in January to February."

"Oh, the moose just throws away his hat!" David can't understand that.

His brother knows even more: "Yes, and the moose weighs up to 800 kilograms."

"My goodness! Look, he has a wide upper lip. That's strange", David thinks.

"The moose is the largest of the deer species", Dennis knows, "and it is the symbol of Sweden."

"Oh, we are in Sweden. Where is this country?" David wants to know.

His brother is happy to answer this question: "Sweden is in the north. It borders the Kattegat, Norway, Finland and the Baltic Sea. The island of Gotland and the island of Öland belong to Sweden and there are many other islands here as well."

"Fine, fine." David continues to watch the moose.

After a while, Dennis would like to travel further. "Would you like to get to know the capital of Sweden? This is Stockholm."

"Sure", David replies, and so the two travel to Stockholm.

"Stockholm has been the king's residence since 1643. Stockholm is also the largest city in Scandinavia", says Dennis, "the queen is from Germany and her name is Silvia."

"What language do they speak in Sweden?" asks David timidly.

"The national language is Swedish. For example, God dag means hello."

"Seeing and hearing a lot makes you hungry, doesn't it?" David grins mischievously.

"Yes, yes, there are some delicious things to eat. For example, Köttbullar, these are meatballs. Or Sill, that's herring. There is also graved lax, raw marinated salmon. As a dessert there is Kanelbullar. These are cinnamon rolls. Kanelbullar is made from yeast dough, cardamom, milk, flour, butter and cinnamon (kanel) and topped with granulated sugar."

"Then I take Köttbullar, that sounds funny", and that's how the little sweet tooth smacks his meatballs.

Dennis decides for Kanelbullar, he loves sweets.

David liked it very much and he wipes the leftovers from his mouth. He lies down in the midday sun with relish.

And Dennis lies down next to him.

After a nap, they continue to travel.

"Bye Sweden."

Norway

A little boy casts a fishing net. "Good Morning!" the blond boy calls out friendly.

"Hello! What's your name?" David asks curiously.

"I am Oscar." The boy with the bright blue eyes greets the two cats with a smile. Oscar would like to know: "Are you tourists?"

David and Dennis nod. "Yes. We would like to know more about the country."

"Of course", Oscar is happy to provide information. "You are in Norway. This is in Scandinavia. The country borders Sweden to the east, Finland to the north-east and Russia."

Full of enthusiasm, he continues: "There are a lot of fjords here."

David furrows his eyebrows and thinks: "Fjords? What is it?"

"A fjord stretches far inland and is formed by valley glaciers that flow down from their source area, the cirque, through river valleys that have been formed. The most famous fjord is the Geirangerfjord and has been a UNESCO World Heritage Site since 2005. It is northeast of Bergen and northwest of Oslo, the capital of Norway." Oscar raves about the country in which he lives.

David looks at the fishing net Oscar is holding. "And what are you doing with this thing?"

"My father and uncle are fishermen. Our family has made a living from fishing for several generations", Oscar proudly reports.

"Is that how you make money to live on?" Dennis asks the little boy.

Oscar nods and shows the fish already caught. "Yes, of course, that's fine. There are cod, herring, haddock, mackerel, cod and salmon in the boat."

"That's great." David is happy and already thinking about the next meal.

"Hm, I like to try a fish", and David already has a piece in his mouth. "Yummy", he smacks.

Dennis would like to know more about the country and its people.

Oscar is happy to give him more information.
"Spitsbergen is Norway's largest island and belongs to the eponymous archipelago in the Arctic Ocean. The North Cape, for example, rises steeply out of the Arctic Ocean. It is about 514 kilometers north of the Arctic Circle. In summer there is the so-called midsummer night for about two and a half months. That means the sun doesn't go down. In winter, on the other hand, the sun does not rise above the horizon for about two and a half months, not even during the day."

Dennis listens carefully. "That all sounds very interesting."

David also agrees and nods before he eats his last fish leftovers.

"Do people in Norway also do sports?" Dennis asks.

"Yes, of course. Winter sports in particular are very popular. Skiing for example. We have a great ski resort, that is Holmenkollen. 1994 are the XVII. Olympic Winter Games held in Lillehammer."

Suddenly David's stomach growls. Unmistakable!

"Do you still have an appetite?" Dennis asks his brother.

Oscar laughs. "There are other dishes, for example lutefisk, which is a traditional fish dish. It's a typical Christmas meal. Lutefisk means lye fish and is made in a lye of birch ash."

David doesn't think twice. "No thanks, I've eaten so much fish." Secretly he thinks: "No, a fish lying in lye like this. Uuh, I don't like that."

After the long lecture, David is tired. He opens his mouth wide and yawns. Dennis laughs. He would have been surprised if his brother didn't think about a nap.

Together with Oscar, the two cats enjoy the warming rays of the sun. The fresh air is good and David is already snoring. After this little break, David and Dennis move on to the next country.

"Ha det" means goodbye in Norwegian.

Denmark

"Who is this?" David stands on the waterfront of Copenhagen, the capital of Denmark.

"This is the little mermaid", explains Dennis, "she is 1.25 meters tall and is called "den lille Havfrue!" in Danish."

David has a few wrinkles in the middle of his forehead and thinks: "Why isn't the lady in the water? That's what mermaids do, right? Although, she is a bronze figure."

Dennis nods and continues: "She is the model for the fairytale character of the same name by Hans Christian Andersen, a Danish poet."

"Ah, I've heard that before", David smiles and is glad he knows something too.

Then he discovers something else. "Look, there are huge ships." Delighted, David runs to the nearest estuary.

"Watch out you fall!", his brother calls anxiously.

"Don't worry, brother, I'll be careful. I know that you have to be very careful on the water."

The two brothers take care of each other.

"The ships are large ferries that go to the Baltic Sea island of Bornholm. Huge cruise ships dock here, taking people to their holiday destinations. Copenhagen is a port city and the port is also called Nyhavn", reports Dennis.

"Great, it must be fun to be on a ship like this." The little cat would love that.

Suddenly a little girl is standing next to him.

"Goddag."

The two cats answer friendly: "Goddag."

David suspects that this means hello in Danish. "Who are you?" he asks curiously.

"My name is Sofie", replies the little one in the pink dress.

David and Dennis sniff Sofie. "Oh, you smell good."

The little David holds his nose in the wind.

"Tak, ah, I mean thank you", Sofie stammers shyly.

"Are you going on a sightseeing tour in Copenhagen?" she asks and offers to show them the city.

The two brothers agree: "You're welcome to do that."

"Over there is the Amalienborg Palace. The Queen lives here with her family. It`s the residence of the royal family."

Sofie points to a building in the middle of the city. "The focal point of this square is an equestrian statue of Frederick V, long ago he was King of Denmark."

David and Dennis are impressed.

They go on and come in front of Copenhagen Central Station.

"There is the Tivoli. This is one of the oldest amusement parks in the world." Sofie points to the sea of flowers and the fountain. An amusement park in the middle of the city. Great.

Dennis thinks it's wonderful.

His brother discovers a small shop with food stuff. "Smørrebrød", he grins, "that sounds funny."

His brother knows what that is. "Smørrebrød is thin brown bread with a lot of fish, meat or eggs. Practically a hot dog in Danish."

But the cinnamon cake is for the little sweet tooth Dennis. "Hm delicious!"

Sofie has to go to school. She is writing a math paper.

"Mathematics? No thank you. I don't like numbers. But you have to learn that", David grudgingly admits.

David and Dennis say goodbye to Sofie.

"It was very nice in Denmark. Farewell, goodbye."

Germany

Germany has 16 federal states. These are Baden-Württemberg, Bavaria, Berlin, Brandenburg, Bremen, Hamburg, Hesse, Mecklenburg-Western Pomerania, Lower Saxony, North Rhine-Westphalia, Rhineland-Palatinate, Saarland, Saxony, Saxony-Anhalt, Schleswig-Holstein and Thuringia.

Berlin is not only a federal state, but also the capital of Germany. The 9 neighboring countries are Denmark, Poland, the Czech Republic, Austria, Switzerland, Luxembourg, France, Belgium and the Netherlands.

David and Dennis live in this country. They live here with their cat mom and cat grandma.

Today the two cats are visiting the capital Berlin. "Wow, that's a huge building", David looks fascinated at the many columns.

Dennis is also very impressed. "This is the Brandenburg Gate and is modeled on the Acropolis in Athens. The Brandenburg Gate is a very popular sight in Germany."

Both pass through the columns. The gate has five passageways. "It's great that you can walk through here." David jumps happily from one pillar to the other.

Suddenly he stops and looks up. "There's a lady on the gate! Who is this?"

"This is the goddess of victory, Victoria. She rode the horse and cart into town to bring peace and prosperity.

But that was a long time ago. This sight is also called Quadriga", explains Dennis.

"Great." David turns and sees another statue that is gold in color. "And who is this?"

Dennis is also enthusiastic about this monument. "This is the Victory Column and again the goddess of victory, Victoria. There are 285 steps that lead to a viewing platform."

"Super. There is a lot to see here. And there's another big tower over there."

Of course, Dennis knows what that is. "Ah, this is the television tower. It stands on Alexanderplatz, which is also affectionately known as Alex. There is a world clock here, the so-called Urania. It is meant to represent the world. 148 cities of the world are on this clock. There are different times all over the world."

"Oh, that's exciting." David would like to know what time it is in the UK right now.

Dennis explains to him that the time in Great Britain is always one hour less than in Germany. "For example, the time on the east coast in New York is 6 hours behind the German time. San Francisco on the west coast of America is even 17 hours behind."

"Interesting." David continues to stroll down the street. "I'm hungry again now!" He smiles mischievously at his brother.

On the next street corner they find the famous currywurst. "Hmm, I'll try that. Smells delicious." He likes the currywurst with French fries and mayonnaise.

"But the food isn't healthy", Dennis notes with concern.

"Sure, I know", grins David, "but you can eat something like that every now and then, right?"

"Yes", Dennis also likes the currywurst.

"And what else do they eat in Germany?"

"This is different. Germany has many federal states. For example, people in Bavaria like to eat white sausage with pretzels. Sauerbraten is a delicacy in the Rhineland. People in Swabia like to eat spaetzle, which is noodles. German cuisine has a lot to offer", explains Dennis.

"But now we're back with mom and grandma. I'm sure it tastes good anywhere in the world, but I still like it best at Mom's", David enthuses.

"Yes, mom will be waiting for us", Dennis adds affectionately. "It was nice to go on a world tour in our dreams."

"But we have one more important thing to explain at the end. In our thoughts we traveled around the world. It was all exciting and very interesting. We also rode with friendly people in dreams, but in real life you shouldn't ride with strangers. But we are sure everyone knows that."

All the best.

Your David

your Dennis

Biography of the author

Anna Maria Kuppe was born in the Rhineland/Germany. She spent her teenage years in the Ruhr area. There she completed an apprenticeship as an industrial clerk. She has been living in the Rhineland again since 1978 and worked for a long time in the accounts department of a language school. She has been retired for a few years. The path to becoming an author was not easy: due to the great grief for her two beloved cats, who died in quick succession, Anna Maria Kuppe wrote down the stories she had experienced with her darlings. This is how her first book came about. Other children's books followed - initially in German. The main characters in these books are her favorites David and Dennis.

In addition to the numerous children's books, novels were also published.

Research

The author has carefully selected the information in this e-book/book in order to give the readers a first impression of the respective countries.

The research is partly based on information from the internet (https://de.wikipedia.org...) and personal travel experiences.

https://de.wikipedia.org/wiki/...

..Holland,...Niederländische Küche...Amsterdam,...Paleis_Noordeinde,...Delft,...Belgien,...Brüssel,...Manneken_Pis,...Grand-Place/Grote_Markt,...Atomium,...Küche_in_Brüssel_und_der_Wallonie,...Antwerpen,...Luxemburg,...Luxemburg_(Stadt),...Luxemburgische_Küche...Österreich,...Wien,...Wiener_Prater,...Österreichische_Küche,...Schweiz,...Bernhardiner,...Matterhorn,...Rheinfall,...Schweizer_Küche,...Paris,...Eiffelturm,...Montmartre,...Arc_de_Triomphe_de_l'Étoile,...Französische_Küche,...Madrid,...Almudena-Kathedrale,...Puerta_del_Sol,...Flamenco,...Spanische_Küche,...Portugal,...Lissabon,...Linie_28E_der_Straßenbahn_Lissabon,...Torre_de_Belém,...Portugiesische_Küche,...Rom,...Pisa,...Griechenland,...Athen,...Bouzouki,...Griechische_Küche,...Südafrika,...Kapstadt,...Tafelberg_(Südafrika),...Kruger-Nationalpark,...Südafrikanische_Küche,...Taj_Mahal,...Indien,...Thail,...Peking,...Chinesische_Mauer,...Hongkong,...Victoria_Towers,...Victoria_Peak_(Hongkong),...Chinesische_Küche,...Australien,...Sydney_Opera_House,...Great_Barrier_Reef,...Australische_Küche,...Neuseeland,...Wellington,...Māori,...Kiwis,...Tongariro-Nationalpark,...Jade,...Neuseeländische_Küche,...Samoa,...Apia,...Mulivai-Kathedrale,...Wappen_Samoas,...Mexiko,...Yucatán_(Halbinsel),...Poncho,...Sombrero,...Maya,...Torre_Latinoamericana,...Panflöte,...Mexikanische_Küche,...Brasilien,...Zuckerhut_(Felsen),...Cristo_Redentor_(Rio_de_Janeiro),...Copacabana_(Rio_de_Janeiro),...Brasilianische_Küche,...Fidschi,...Tomatinvi,...Vereinigte_Staaten,...ABC-Staaten,...Freiheitsstatue,...Los_Angeles,...Golden_Gate_Bridge,...Küche_der_Vereinigten_Staaten,...Kanada,...Ottawa,...Niagarafälle,...Rocky_Mountains,...Yellowstone-Nationalpark,...Flagge_Kanadas,...Kategorie:Kanadische_Küche,...Irland,...Dublin,...Phoenix_Park,...Nationalparks_in_Irland,...Ring_of_Kerry,...Wappen_der_Republik_Irland,...St._Patrick's_Day,...Irische_Küche,...Vereinigtes_Königreich,...London,...Big_Ben,...Buckingham_Palace,...Britische_Küche,...Britische_Teekultur,...Schottland,...Edinburgh,...Forth_Bridge,...Loch_Ness,...Highlands,...Highland_Games,...Sackpfeife_(Musikinstrument),...Kilt,...Shortbread,...Haggis,...Schweden,...Nationalparks_in_Schweden,...Elch,...Stockholm,...Schwedische_Küche,...Köttbullar,...Kanelbulle,...Norwegen,...Fjord,...Spitzbergen_(Inselgruppe),...Nordkap,...Holmenkollen,...Lutefisk,...Dänemark,...Kopenhagen,...Kleine_Meerjungfrau,...Nyhavn,...Schloss_Amalienborg,...Tivoli_(Kopenhagen),...Hans_Christian_Andersen,...Dänische_Küche,...Deutschland,...Berlin,...Brandenburger_Tor,...Berliner_Siegessäule,...Berliner_Fernsehturm,...Weltzeituhr_(Alexanderplatz),...Deutsche_Küche